The Pot
with a Dot

Pam Scheunemann

Consulting Editor, Diane Craig, M.A./Reading Specialist

Published by ABDO Publishing Company, 4940 Viking Drive, Edina, Minnesota 55435.

Printed in the United States.

Credits
Edited by: Pam Price
Curriculum Coordinator: Nancy Tuminelly
Cover and Interior Design and Production: Mighty Media
Photo Credits: AbleStock

Library of Congress Cataloging-in-Publication Data

Scheunemann, Pam, 1955-
    The pot with a dot / Pam Scheunemann.
        p. cm. -- (First rhymes)
    Includes index.
    ISBN 1-59679-511-5 (hardcover)
    ISBN 1-59679-512-3 (paperback)
        1. English language--Rhyme--Juvenile literature. I. Title. II. Series.
PE1517.S444 2005
808.1--dc22

                                                                    2005048036

SandCastle™ books are created by a professional team of educators, reading specialists, and content developers around five essential components that include phonemic awareness, phonics, vocabulary, text comprehension, and fluency. All books are written, reviewed, and leveled for guided reading and early intervention reading, and designed for use in shared, guided, and independent reading and writing activities to support a balanced approach to literacy instruction.

Let Us Know

After reading the book, SandCastle would like you to tell us your stories about reading. What is your favorite page? Was there something hard that you needed help with? Share the ups and downs of learning to read. We want to hear from you! To get posted on the ABDO Publishing Company Web site, send us e-mail at:

sandcastle@abdopub.com

SandCastle Level: Beginning

-ot

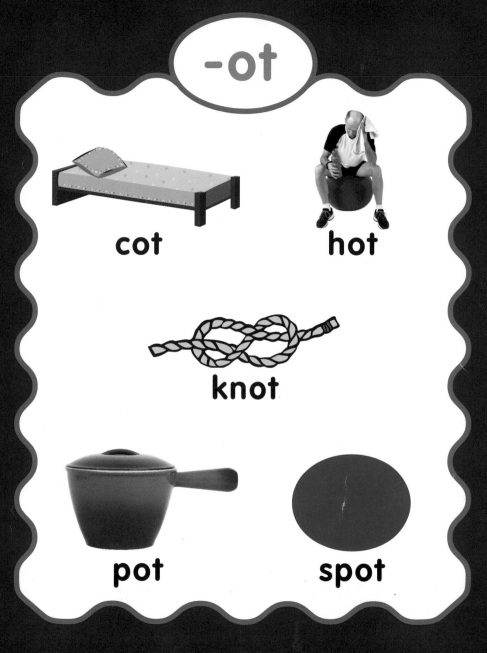

cot

hot

knot

pot

spot

Here is a .

He is  .

Look at the .

This is a .

This is a .

The cot is soft.

The man is hot.

The rope is
tied in a knot.

The pot is red.

The spot is blue.

The Pot
with a Dot

Look at the
big, blue spot.

On the big, blue spot,
there is a cot.

18

On the cot
on the big, blue spot
is a rope with a knot.

Next to the knot
on the cot
that is on the
big, blue spot
is a pot
with a dot.

Steve saw the pot
with a dot
next to the knot
on top of the cot
on the big, blue spot.

"Oh my," he said,
"that pot is hot!"

About SandCastle™

A professional team of educators, reading specialists, and content developers created the SandCastle™ series to support young readers as they develop reading skills and strategies and increase their general knowledge. The SandCastle™ series has four levels that correspond to early literacy development in young children. The levels are provided to help teachers and parents select the appropriate books for young readers.

Emerging Readers
(no flags)

Beginning Readers
(1 flag)

Transitional Readers
(2 flags)

Fluent Readers
(3 flags)

These levels are meant only as a guide. All levels are subject to change.

To see a complete list of SandCastle™ books and other nonfiction titles from ABDO Publishing Company, visit **www.abdopub.com** or contact us at:
4940 Viking Drive, Edina, Minnesota 55435 • 1-800-800-1312 • fax: 1-952-831-1632